Victoria
Happy Birthday
Love Aunty Julia, Catherine & Lucy
& Robert
XXXX
1982

Traveller's Joy, Vagabond's Friend,
Timeless weeds of the wayside,
Wild garden of the wayfarer,
That enhances his wanderings.

Traveller's Joy

Gypsy's Baccy
Clematis vitaba

To the memory of Augustus

This book is dedicated to the memory of
a 'romantic wayfarer' fondly remembered in his
wild garden, who enhanced many a pause in our
wanderings, the 'Romany Rai', Augustus John,
for whose kind encouragement I am ever
most grateful.

First published in Great Britain 1980 by
Granada Publishing Limited
Frogmore, St Albans, Herts. AL2 2NF
and
Gallery Five Limited
14 Ogle Street, London W1P 7LG
Illustrations Copyright © 1978, 1979, 1980 Gallery Five Limited
Text Copyright © 1980 Gallery Five Limited
Layout by Daphne Mattingly

Printed in Great Britain by W. S. Cowell Limited, Ipswich

Traveller's Joy

by

BESHLIE

Granada and Gallery Five

INTRODUCTION

I hope this little book will help you to remember the names of some of the weeds of the wayside. Every plant has its own Latin botanical name, and at the end of the book I have tried to explain how these work. But some also have lovely, some curious and some funny names given to them by ordinary people who spent their lives passing along the highways and byways and working in the meadows alongside the flowers. Balm-of-the-warrior's-wound, fair-maid-of-France, hobble-gobbles, kitty-come-down-the-lane-jump-up-and-kiss-me, higey-pidgy and humpy-scrumples; names like these show how much the plants were once held in regard and affection. Cannot we do the same?

Most hard-working country folk either could not read at all or had little time and money to spare for books. So folk tales, stories, family history and the names and uses of plants were handed down by word of mouth. Knowledge of herbs and husbandry was taught by demonstration as son followed father in the same occupation. Sometimes the likeness of useful plants was embroidered on samplers, which were a sample of the sewer's skill in needlework, and household linen; or else carved on chair backs, stools and church pews.

Before the days of picture books, films or television, when storytellers were in great demand, plants played a major part in old customs, superstitions and magic. Once witches were not thought of as undesirable neighbours, they practised their black or white art openly; people respected their superior knowledge of herbs and purchased their potions. A person would ask a witch to put an evil spell on an enemy, or cure a friend. Certain plants soon gained a reputation as good cures, others were thought to be bad.

But witchcraft was just one element of country life which provided popular names for plants that survive to the present day. It's my hope that this book, as well as being informative about some of my favourite plants, will also lead the reader to an interest in some of the old country ways from which spring many of the plants' fascinating and lovely popular names.

GYPSY ROSES

Once, when I was encamped with other Travellers on a roadside in Hampshire, we were making 'gypsy roses' from crepe paper wired on to leafy twigs and dipped into pots of hot candle wax melted on the ornate Queenie stoves. In the summer, this verge used to be full of scabious, the original gypsy rose. Now they barely have time to flower before they suffer the fate of most wayside flowers and are cut down by a council verge cutter.

At one time, cultivated flowers grew only in the gardens of the rich; cottagers grew practical flowers such as herbs. Flowers to decorate the church for weddings, May Day festivities and garlands to hang around house and stable doors were all picked from the fields. It was quite usual for people to wear fresh flowers round their heads, hats or in posies pinned to their clothing. This is a tradition which is carried on today by Morris Dancers, but if you examine their hats too closely you will see that many of the flowers are made of plastic! Scabious is also called blue bonnets.

When I helped my grandmother decorate the font of our church for the christening of my cousin, we included many wild flowers. Her grandmother had told her mugwort, ivy and corn marigold brought extra blessings upon a wedding or christening.

Field Scabious
Knautia arvensis

POLICEMAN'S HELMET

One of the most remarkable stories of an escaped prisoner is that of this slightly fearsome-looking balsam. Well over a hundred years ago, this foreigner was introduced as an exotic conservatory plant. Owing to the amazing distance the catapulted seed is flung, it soon germinated in the gardens, finally escaping to thrive on our cold river banks. There is an old mill house in Oxfordshire, where the miller's daughter, a friend of mine, lives. Every year, this strange flower would arise and grow with the rapidity of an annual which, in its native land, reaches nine or ten feet. Then one year, after heavy floods, it did not appear beside the gypsywort and watermint where previously it had dropped its flowers to float like fairy boats among the ducklings in the mill pond. A year or so later it reappeared.

On a river bank near Upper Dicker in Sussex, I found a plant of the lovely brilliant orange balsam, originating from North America. Shallow gravel-bars in the River Usk and driftwood islands in a Llangurig river I have found covered with showy yellow flowers of touch-me-not which has long downward curving spurs.

These balsams share the remarkable habit of bombarding any man, dog or bird who touches them with a fusillade of seeds; this hasty gesture accounts for the Latin name *Impatiens* and the nickname 'jumping jacks'.

Indian Balsam
Impatiens glandulifera

BRIDE'S BOUQUET

Bride's bouquet has a very sturdy main stem, from which the long branches, covered with thorns, hang down in rainbow-shaped arches, each supporting numbers of delicate pink 'saucers', rather like a florist's arrangement of 'hanging' flowers for a bride to carry. Another popular name is hedgie-pedges. Being an inquisitive child, I once asked a gypsy who stopped on our family farm once a year to pick the apples, why she hung her washing upon the hedge to dry. She answered, 'Because it is nature's clothes-line my dear'. The memory of her showing me the 'hedge-pegs', namely the hooked thorns of the briar, returned many times during later years, when I too was to use this convenient method while leading an itinerant life.

It is worth searching waste land, especially old railway embankments where there has been no hedge trimming, to experience the breathtaking sight of a fine specimen, rampant in full summer glory, growing as nature intended.

The wild rose often carries a curious 'bloom', a round furry growth, often fiery red that is not a flower but the self-made home of the larva of a tiny gall wasp. Like the country children I knew, I called it Robin's pin-cushion.

Wild Rose
Rosa canina

DRUMMER BOYS

One of the sad things about a life on the move is that when much-loved birds or animals die, you cannot 'lay them to rest' in some corner of the garden, where, as you tend the flowers, you feel they are not entirely separated from you.

Brown knapweed reminds me of two such companions. Wolsey, my beautiful Virginian Cardinal, a bird of magnificent scarlet feather, loved this plant's seeds, which helped him maintain his splendid colour. When he died, I left him under an oak tree on which his cage had often hung in the sun, by the side of a Wiltshire lane.

Oddly enough, it was here that our Welsh cob, when taking a barrel-top waggon downhill, stopped and refused to move. At this point, the banks were very steep and the road so narrow that the wheel-hubs just missed the sides. After a minute or so, when the fly terrets and bells had stopped jingling, we too heard a strange noise. Glancing upwards we saw cables overhead, whining and humming in the wind: electric pylons had been erected since we last journeyed that way. After reassuring her we reached the bottom with rather more speed than usual.

Once this horse cured herself of a hoof complaint by eating knapweed; so the plant always reminds me of the stout-hearted animal, the best waggon horse we ever had.

Brown Knapweed
Centaurea nemoralis

COUNTRY LAWYERS

'You bin eatin' bluey-brambles 'stead o' cuttin' the dashels,' said Old Riner, who worked (when he wasn't asleep in the wheelbarrow) for my grandfather, to Gilbert, the gardener's boy. A translation of this is 'You have been eating dewberries instead of cutting down the thistles'. The bloom on the fruit, from which no dewberry can escape, prompts the name blue bramble; whilst the white flowers and black fruit, like white wigs and black gowns, have led to the name country lawyers.

Old Riner was never heard to refer to any wild flowers other than by rustic names. Of my grandmother's 'cultivated' garden flowers, he denied any knowledge, other than to call them contemptuously, 'they finicky flowers'. Should he ever be forced into contact with 'the garden', he speedily returned to 'the yard', a large area of bricks laid on edge, fronting the stables and the forge, where, in defiance of orders, he allowed weeds to grow. Those especially tall had a favoured position around his barrow, which, handles resting on the ground, afforded him a seat for eating hunks of bread and cheese. To my fascination he severed the cheese straight into his mouth with a hoof-paring knife!

Dewberry
Rubus caesius

BLUE BASINS

Here is a plant with an easy name to remember. The seed vessel takes the form of a long pod with a pointed tip; this protrudes from the rounded calyx which resembles a bird's head, which in turn is joined to a delicate curving stem or neck. The whole thing bears a likeness to the beak, head and neck of a crane.

Part of its Latin name, *pratense*, means 'of meadows' and this most showy of the cranesbills (excepting perhaps the vivid pink *Geranium sanguineum*) would prefer to grow in the meadows. But many plants are ousted to the roadsides, bringing a welcome blue to verges where there are relatively few blue flowers. A close look will show delicate red veins in the petals, and that this coloration is present throughout the plant. Many of the geranium family share this characteristic, and some, like the shining cranesbill, have leaves and stems which redden considerably, making the plant conspicuous.

The blooms seem to float upon the plant like fragile basins, hence one of its popular names. The leaves at the base of the plant, which can be quite enormous, turn bright yellow and red in the autumn, so that the plant then carries the colours of green, yellow, red and blue. No wonder it is known also as 'gypsy'.

Meadow Cranesbill
Geranium pratense

FLIPPERTY GIBBET

From the imposing hollyhock to the self-effacing least mallow, the
Malvaceae family gives us a lively display of blooms of various shades,
shapes and sizes, not to mention texture! Coming across these bright
flowers flaunting themselves with such a jaunty, flippant air, one can
easily understand the plant's common name. It is a name I have good
reason to remember, since it was once given to me by a kindly country
doctor who had the unenviable task of putting the fingers of both my
hands back together again after an accident. 'Where's my little flip-
perty gibbet?' he said, perching me upon his desk where I was allowed
to unravel the painful-to-remove bandages in my own time.

    The common mallow, fairy cheese as it's sometimes called,
sprawls across corners of rough ground, claiming a short-lease of
tenancy at the top of mounds of road-builders' rubble, or enhancing
a wild 'herbaceous border' along a country lane. The circular cluster
of seeds bears a resemblance to round cheeses.

Common Mallow
Malva sylvestris

PLUM PUDDING

As the outer covering of white campion's seed vessels peels away, it reveals a shiny brown pod, crinkled at the top like a plum pudding after the cook has peeled off the cloth in which it has been boiled. Hence the popular country name: plum puddings with various fillings were once part of a countryman's staple diet.

The campion's seeds rattle in the pod when ripe, and cause it to be known as cowbell. The pods being wide open at the top, care has to be taken when gathering them for cage-birds. Many insects like the seeds, and earwigs can often be found in the pods enjoying their daytime nap. The mule-birds which I breed (crossing a canary hen with a goldfinch) are particularly fond of campions, catchflys and chickweed, all members of the same family.

After sundown, the dazzling white flowers remain open almost luminous under the moon. It is one of the best flowers to attract moths, which, as they emerge from hiding in the tall hay grass, drift in vast numbers towards the plant. I have many times caught the beautiful crimson-red and yellow-green elephant hawkmoth visiting campions; because their vivid colouring is such an exact match, they seem to prefer the red campion.

White Campion
Silene alba

SCHOOL BELLS

I think it is true to say that you have little difficulty remembering injustices done to you. At school, during 'general knowledge', I was asked 'what is campanology?' to which I replied, 'The art of harebell ringing'. The mistress, unaware that the flower's generic name is *Campanula* (meaning little bell), failed to see the connection or appreciate my juvenile wit, and sent me to the bottom of the class!

In Scotland, bluebells are known as wild hyacinths, and it is the harebell which is 'the bluebell of Scotland'. The long specific name *rotundifolia* simply means round leaf. This may seem rather surprising, since however closely you may examine a bunch of harebells, you will only see leaves the reverse of round: indeed, they are long and thin, blending with grass leaves. However, at the base of the stems you may find one or two very old round leaves which usually die off when the plant begins to grow its slender leaves.

The hairlike stems and thin leaves keep it so well hidden in the grasses that a bank which gives no indication of the existence of any flowers at all can be blowing the next day with these fragile blooms of gossamer beauty. Delicate as a butterfly's wing, the slightest breeze nudges their papery bells into a magical rustling.

Harebell
Campanula rotundifolia

LADY'S SUNSHADE

You will not have to search very diligently to find the lesser bind-weed. Once established next to a kerb, many yards of the wayside are soon edged with a narrow ribbon of pink flowers upturned to the sun, almost petal to petal. If you examine the back of the flowers you will see a thicker stripe of deeper pink which is almost like a false calyx and which strengthens the flower in much the same way as the ribs of a parasol. This contributes towards the popular name of lady's sunshade. The slightest change in the weather causes the flowers to close up so that the thin petal-fabric is safely folded within the tough pink stripe.

Lesser bindweed or gypsy's hat can be a nuisance to the farmer, tenacious stems and roots ensuring an everlasting footing since even a small portion, if severed by the plough, can create a new plant. The bindweed twines up the stems of grain or grass, and reaching the top, waves about until it is able to catch hold of a neighbouring blade, thus binding the corn together. The true bindweeds all twine in an anti-clockwise direction.

Bindweed is the food plant of the Convolvulus Hawk Moth caterpillar, a beautiful nocturnal moth sometimes seen flying during the day. It can feed on-the-wing like a hummingbird.

Lesser Bindweed
Convolvulus arvensis

WITCH'S FINGERS

This member of the rose family, also called golden blossom, bears flowers which resemble those of a yellow rose; they are quite pretty, with the bright green calyx showing through between the petals like its relative the silverweed. It is easily seen how the popular name witch's fingers came about, with the leaves forming a hand. People believed witches used the plant.

Creeping cinquefoil can quickly colonize a large area of ground by means of its long tough runners which form new plants at frequent intervals, like the strawberry. It is a useful weed for paths where its decorative leaves and cheerful flowers give rather better value than insignificant-flowered weeds or those which have wind-borne seeds that are only too anxious to leave the path for the garden.

It is worth remembering that plants always spread towards the light (as a rough guide, towards where the sun is at midday). So if you want a path covered with eye-catching cinquefoil, plant the first root as far away from the light as possible.

Creeping Cinquefoil
Potentilla reptans

TRUMPET FLOWER

In Elizabethan times, honeysuckle was used to make bowers, where people could sit shaded from the sun, and enjoy the cool breezes filtering through the lacy boughs, wafting delicious scent within. It does not take as long as one might suppose to make such a bower: the vines grow quickly, once established. It takes rather longer to locate a suitable root. If you search for one to transplant you will soon feel that it has been growing there for centuries and is firmly rooted!

Recently I made a rustic archway. Sheep had escaped through a hedge and taken with them a strand of a young plant. This lay crushed in the road. I planted it by the archway, it seemed to recover and flourished for a week or two, then appeared to die. This is the time to be patient and not move it; the plants usually recover, sending out new shoots from the root, and the 'dead' vine. The next year, a riot of long arms will spring out, usually at the same time as the 'old' wood is flowering. You can see this in the illustration. Luckily for the honeysuckle, it swiftly recovers from drastic pruning, when it succumbs temporarily to the tractor-driven hedge cutter.

The flower-tubes are too long for bees to pollinate, so the scent becomes heavier towards nightfall, attracting moths and the splendid name 'Pride of the Evening'.

Honeysuckle
Lonicera periclymenum

BOTANICAL NAMES EXPLAINED

As well as its common name, each plant has its own Latin name. The same plant may have had the common name hobble-gobbles in an eastern county and yet was called jack-in-the-box in a western county. People who worked the land spent a lifetime in one place, so plant names remained very local. As names were taught verbally, mistakes occurred; perhaps a grandmother's sight was not too good, or her granddaughter did not take a close enough look at the plant, so often two different but similar flowers were given the same name.

Eventually, botanists began to sort plants into groups, giving them new names, or altering the common name. It was all rather a muddle. New herbals were compiled in an effort to establish a reliable record. A great pioneer of English botany was William Turner, who was born about 1512. It was, however, a Swedish naturalist called Linnaeus who undertook the immense task of classifying systematically the plant and animal world.

Plants were given two names. The first, always beginning with a capital letter is called the generic name and it tells you to what group the plant belongs. You might care to regard this as a 'surname', though it is always printed first. The second name, beginning with a small letter, is called the specific name and it denotes the species in the group, to which the plant belongs. Like a christian name, this can be the same for another plant, but not one in the same group.

The specific name often describes a plant's colour, shape, habit or use. For example, *tintoria* means 'of dyers' and is used for both saw-wort and dyer's greenwood, which give yellow dye, and for woad which makes a blue dye. A great number of wild and garden flowers are named after the person who discovered them, or in honour of some famous botanist. Linnaeus had a little creeping plant named after him. It has small bell-like pink flowers and grows in shady places in eastern Scotland. When recording it in one of his books, having described its rather wizened characteristics, he noted that it was 'named after Linnaeus who resembles it'.

SOME COMMON SPECIFIC NAMES

It's useful to know what some of the Latin specific names mean in English because they often tell us the places and conditions in which the plant can be found growing. For example:

arenaria	in sandy places	*pratense*	in meadows
arvensis	in fields	*repens*	along the ground
byron	among moss	*rupestris*	on rocks
communis	in company	*rusticans*	in the country
collena	on hills	*sativa*	under cultivation
muralis	on walls	*sepium*	in hedgerows
palustris	in marshes	*sylvatica*	in woodlands

Some specific names reveal other characteristics of the plant – its colour, the shape of its leaves, or connection with animals.

alba	white	*lactea*	milky
anserina	of geese	*lathyrus*	pod-bearing
aromatic	sweet-smelling	*oleracea*	edible
canina	of dogs	*rotundifolia*	round-leaved
cala	good	*rubus*	red
cataria	of cats	*spurge*	purging
droseros	dewy	*tremula*	trembling
fragula	fragile	*vulgaris*	common
glutinosa	sticky	*vulneraria*	healing
hirsutum	hairy	*vesca*	weak

Some flowers bear male & female flowers on separate plants. Some are sterile. Flowers are pollinated by bees, moths, butterflies, hoverflies, flies, and wind. In the event of failure by these, they resort to self-pollination. As the insect goes in or out, pollen is rubbed off onto it's head or body, even it's tongue.

COROLLA (PETALS)
Help to attracting insects by bright colours

SCENT WAVES

FILAMENT ('STALK OF STAMEN')

BRIGHT COLOURS

STIGMA which receives pollen (part of the PISTIL)

ANTHER pollen-producing organ

STYLE 'stalk' of stigma. (part of the PISTIL, the female part of flower.)

SHINEY to attract

STAMENS
These are the male part of the flower, producing pollen.

SEPALS
(CALYX, SEPALS AS A WHOLE)
These protect the bud.

Round, square, ridged stems

NECTARY
(PRODUCES NECTAR)

CARPEL
(CONTAINS OVULE)
Female part of flower which is fertilised and produces seed.

HAIRS

LUMINOUS for night

Insects hunting for nectar carry pollen from the male flowers, inside each pollen grain is a germ produced by anthers in the male flowers.

WATER CATCHMENT base of leaf

NODES

PEDICEL (STALK)

SPINES

SEEDPOD

SEEDS or fruit

LEAF SERRATE

OVATE LEAF

BULBIL can break off to form new plant

TENDRIL used to assist climbing some plants use their leaf stems for this.

STEM

new plant

THORN protection

RUNNER (a rooting-shoot)

PALMATE LEAF

LANCEOLATE LEAF

SHOOT for more flowers

MAIN ROOT balances flower

RHIZOME under ground root or stem producing new shoots.

SPIKE of flowers

FOOD STORE

WATER ROOTS
Flowers also use scent to attract insects, some open at night, others only in sunny weather saving themselves for when insects fly.

UMBEL of flowers

WHORL of flowers

TUBE of petals or of calyx can be joined like this.

BUD flower before opening

TAP ROOTS

FOOD ROOTS